To my Timmy & Jerome

COPYRIGHT © 2021
St Shenouda Press

ST SHENOUDA PRESS
8419 Putty Rd,
Putty, NSW, 2330
Sydney, Australia

www.stshenoudapress.com

ISBN 13: 978-0-6451394-5-7

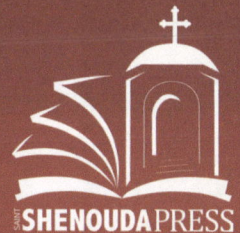

SHENOUDA PRESS

On Sunday we go to church to see Jesus, our king.

It's where we go to raise our voice to Him and sing.

Before we get to church, we read a psalm and pray.

we fast before communion to feel close to God that day.

Candle

Candles remind us of God, who lights up our day.

He guides us and leads us in the right way.

Candles line the alter and where the Bible is read.

They remind us to obey God and trust in what He said.

An orbana is round and has no beginning or end,
It reminds us of Jesus who will always be our friend.

Orbana

When Abouna prays on the orbana it becomes the body of Christ.

It reminds us of His love and all that He sacrificed.

Icon

The icons in church show stories of Jesus and the saints.

With beautiful swirls of color, in many different paints.

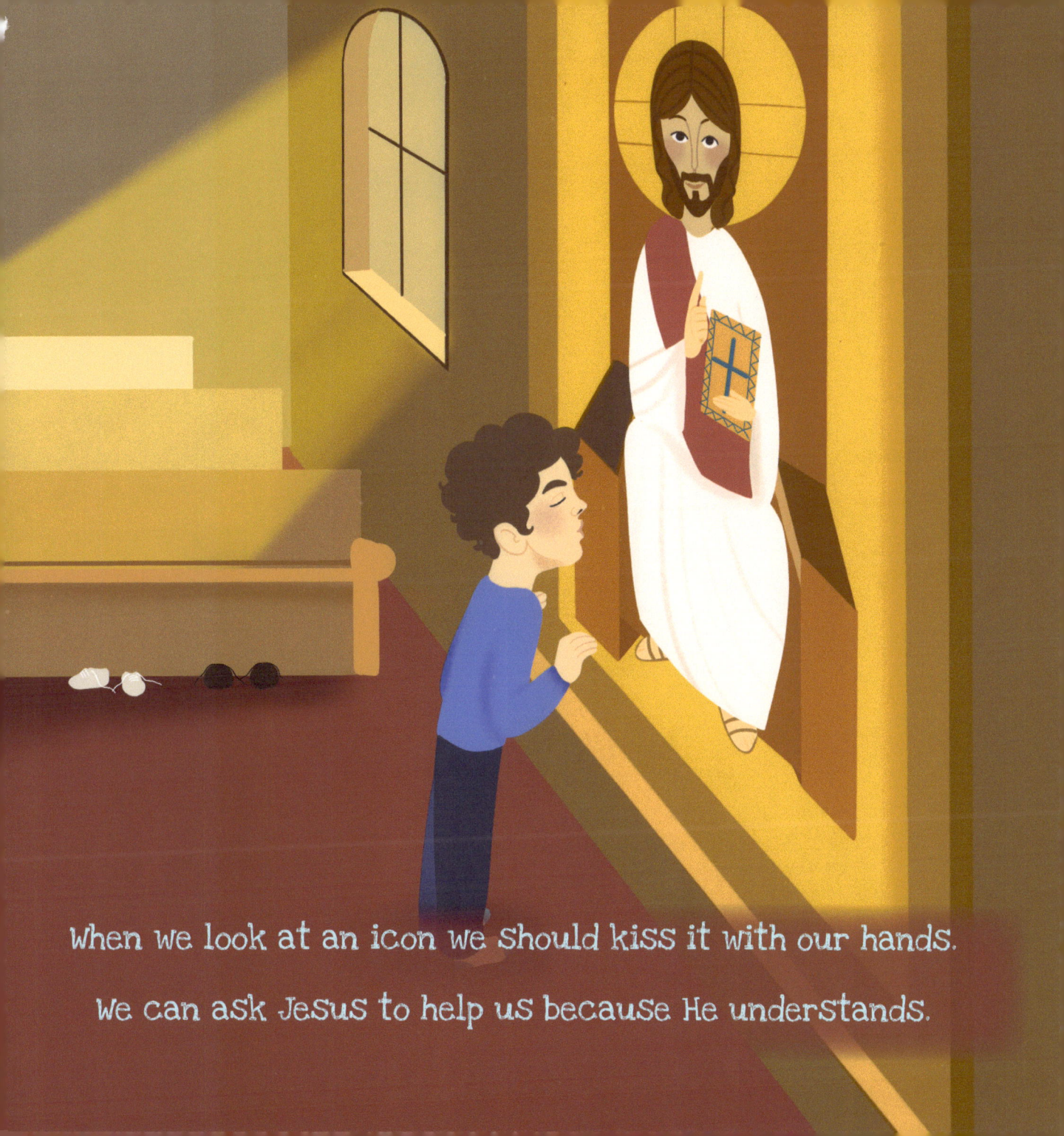

When we look at an icon we should kiss it with our hands.

We can ask Jesus to help us because He understands.

Censer

When Abouna uses the censor, incense fills the air.

It reminds us of God, our Father, who is with us everywhere.

The incense that rises is so beautiful to see.

It carries our prayers to Jesus who always hears me.

Tonia

When Abouna prays the liturgy, he wears a tonya that is white.

He reminds us of God, our Father, who is our guiding light.

The deacons wear a tonya decorated with crosses so bright.

They remind us of angels who watch over us day and night.

Sign of the Cross

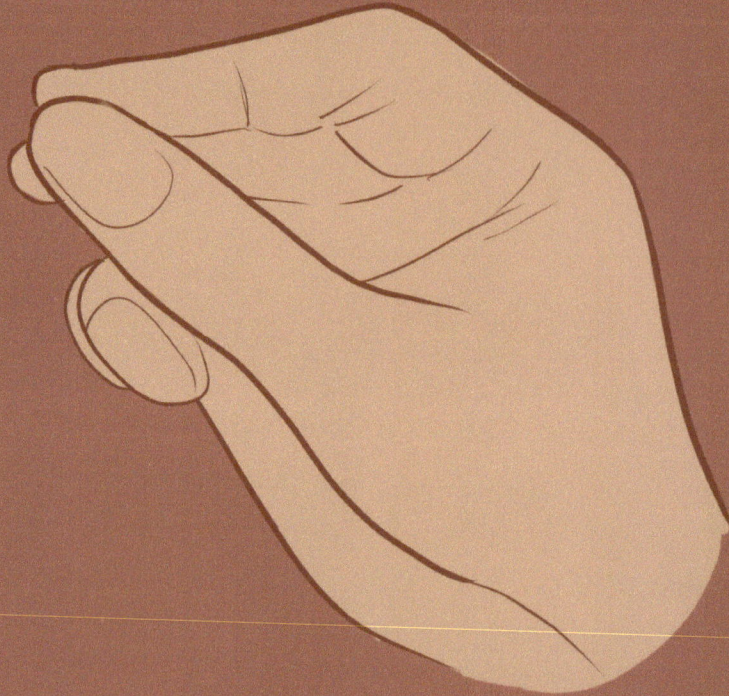

When you want to feel that God is close to you,

Make the sign of the cross, it's easy to do.

We put 3 fingers together, we shut our eyes real tight,

We move our hand up, then down, then left and right.

Liturgical Books

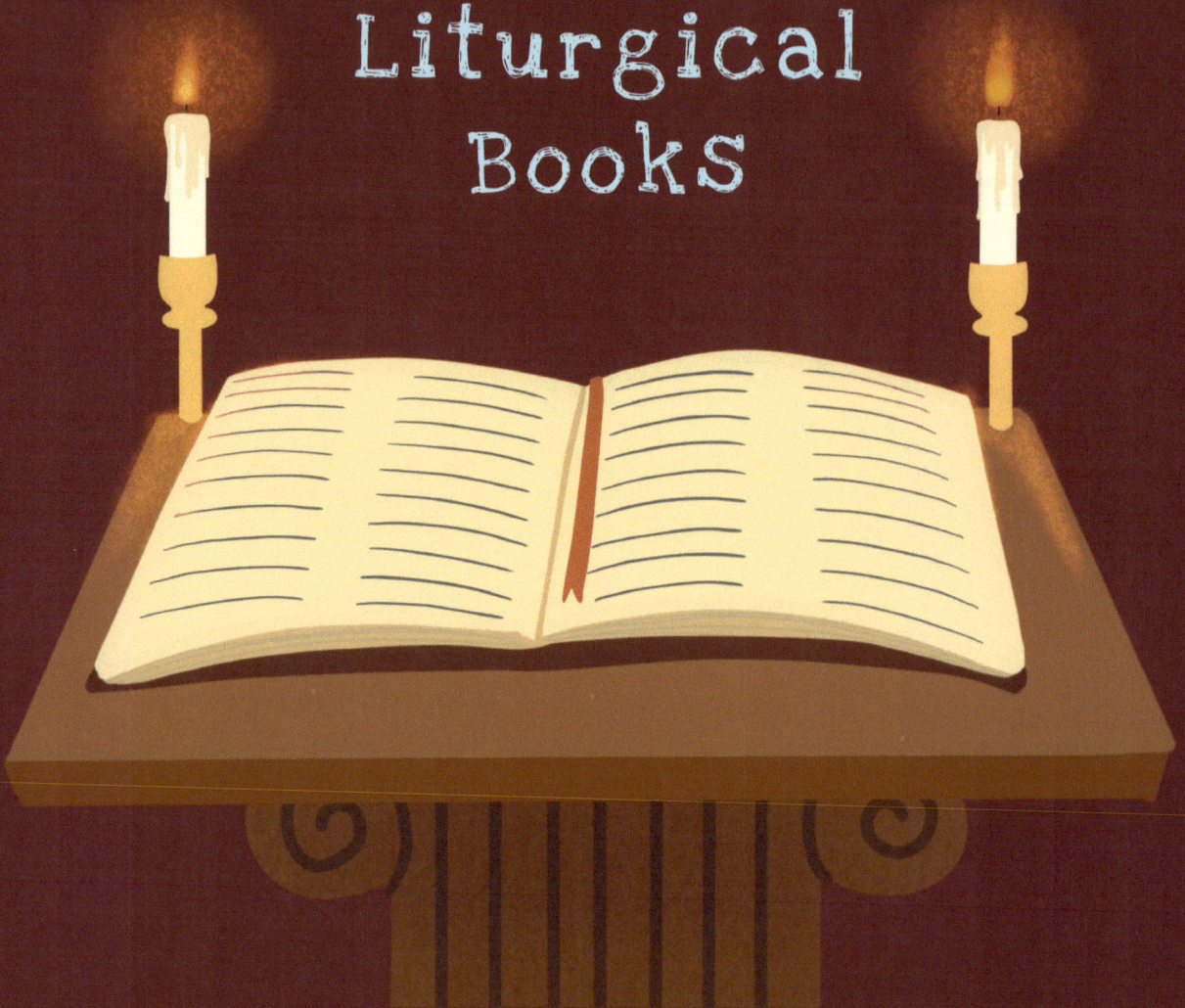

If we want to hear god's voice, the Bible is where to look.

When we read it everyday, it will be our favourite book.

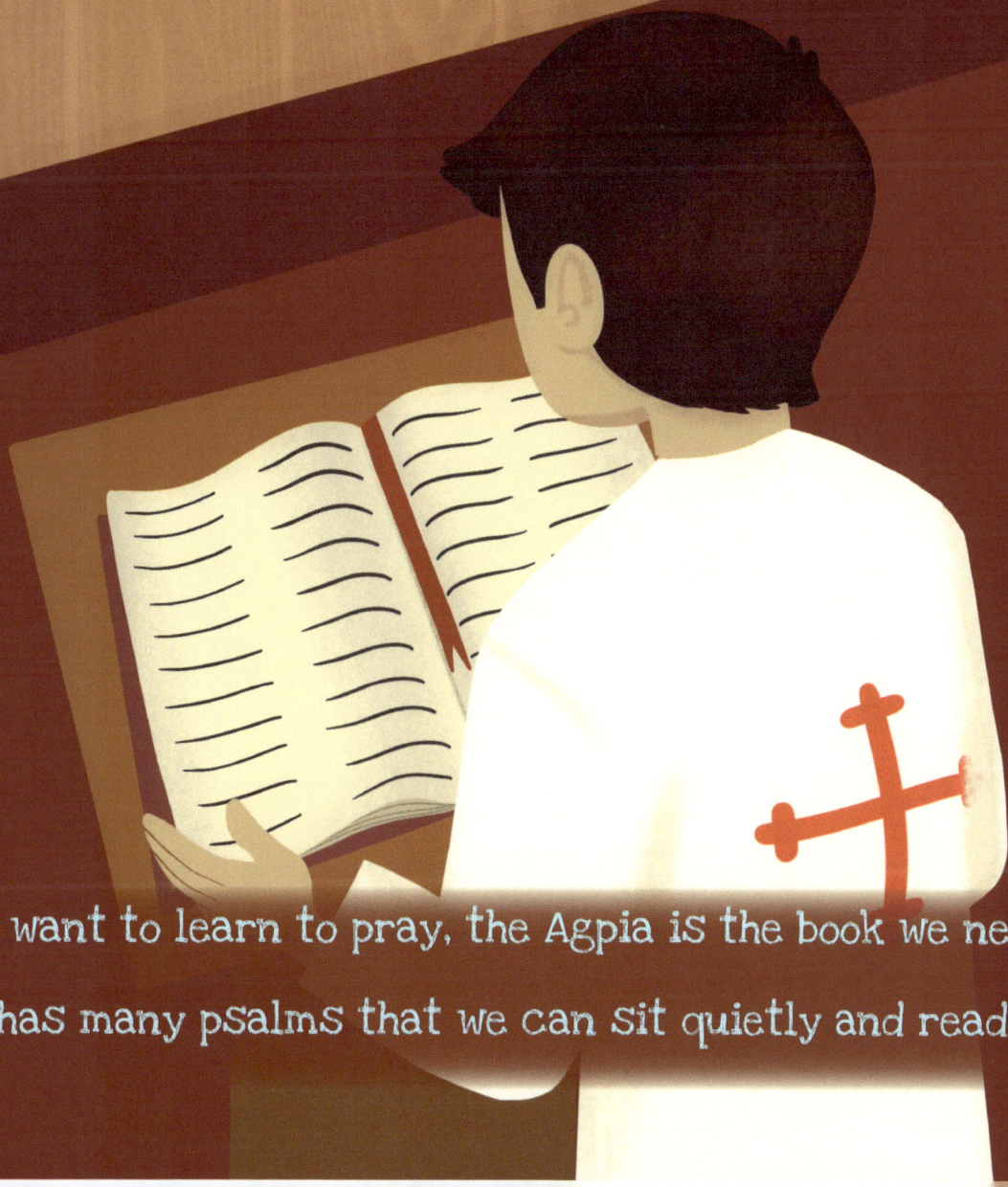

If we want to learn to pray, the Agpia is the book we need.

It has many psalms that we can sit quietly and read.

Cymbals

Triangle

Singing in the liturgy, we praise God for his love.

We follow His journey from birth to His ascension above.

The deacons use instruments when they raise their voice to sing.

They play the cymbals and triangle to praise God as our King.

Being at church with God is amazing and fun.

It feels good to thank God for all that He's done.

And when we're home we should pray every day.

Until we go see God at church again on Sunday.

THE END

www.ingramcontent.com/pod-product-compliance
Lightning Source LLC
Chambersburg PA
CBHW042012080426
42734CB00002B/60